The Englewood Readings

Terence Clarke

Drawings and cover design by Cathleen Daly

Dustbooks
1976

ISBN: 0-913218-29-4 Paper
ISBN: 0-913218-30-8 Cloth

Printed in the United States of America

Library of Congress Cataloging in Publication Data

Clarke, Terence.
The Englewood readings.

(American dust series; no. 5)
Poems.
I. Title.

PS3553.L338E5	811'.5'4	76-8892

ISBN 0-913218-30-8
ISBN 0-913218-29-4 pbk.

"American Dust" Series, No. 5

First Printing, 1976
Published by Dustbooks,
PO Box 1056, Paradise, CA 95969

Grateful acknowledgement is made by the author to the editors of the following magazines, where many of these poems first appeared:
Dryad
Gallery Works
Hyperion
North Country Almanac
Quarry
Wednesday Nights
West Coast Poetry Review

The Englewood Readings was designed by the Mason Street Press, San Francisco.

Contents

Englewood is a ranch located near Redcrest, in the Redwood National Forest of Northern California.

". . .the ax-scented breeze. . . ."
Galway Kinnell

For Cathleen

ENGLEWOOD

Between the forest and the mill,
the houses fall to the ground,
as the orchards do,
sagging more each year
with senility and dead apples.
On Sundays,
the mill is silent.
Only the houses—
small gatherings of grace
and the exchange of pleasantries.
The hammocks and the cocktails
make a feeble point
for peace instead of war.

The barn is jammed with old chickens.
Its tin roof shines in the fog
and keeps the rain off,
the saddles inside
cracking like cups
in an age of uselessness,
of drinks and Sunday dinners.
On Monday, the mill will roar
against its enemies.
Pleasant that patter,
hamburgers and beer
arrest the carnage for a day,
though this response
is a gesture in the blitz.

THE HOMECOMING

Out of work.
An old scenario . . .
broke.
At the store I hold my tongue
when they ask where I've been.
Paris? They'd think I'm hiding out.
Nothing but rain here,
though the rent is free.
I hesitate to say
this represents the fall of man:
crepes suzettes to Redcrest
in one month.
Who loves elegance should stay away.
The mist in winter hardens,
point by point,
as the thermometer descends.

To search within the mud
the root's tip
requires our presence here,
as does the recollection
of July, at 7:40,
when my father-in-law said
"This is the best time of the day."
I removed my shirt
to feel like him the dying warmth.
Not so bad.
This place gives back when asked.
The valley diminishes,
redwoods shrink,
and the push,
the edging forth of an evening,
overwhelms us.

CURLING UP WITH A GOOD BOOK

Dark leaves riveted to the window
demand a case of nerves.
It is a noise evisceral
to the progress of conversations.
My hope for warmth is shaken
for our room is transparent,
the fire blue.
Flames shard beneath the last log
and I am overcome by the failing light
as cold stifles the fire.

So I cut wood at night.
I sweat beneath my coat,
the salt and rain watering the cloth
so that I harden as I dry.
Nothing fatal;
a stiffness in the joints.
But such cold should be reserved,
for explorers
of the Arctic or the poles,
not for sluggish dwellers
in a wet house.

I look round at the fire,
frozen now in my coat.
It crackles, as before,
defying our hope for something new.
So betrayed,
I exchange one Dickens for another
and drowse in my boots.

FOR CATHLEEN

who, deep-bellied, is both my wife and child.
Stuck for appreciations,
I can say only that
you are what I entered
and are what I caused.
As in the colius.
Its red leaves, veined green,
darken thick when healthy.
The earth it enters enters it;
smoothed and held by hedge-green sap,
it slips from root to bloom.

BAPTISMALS

A bit of advice: cut the cord
though aware that my fall
tears the stones from this cliff.
I fall,
as my father fell,
cut under from the moment
of our first embrace.
One day,
you will fall as well.

If I give way,
it will be because you let me go.
The river below will offer baptismals,
the rocks passage—
a good choice for a certain end.
So, go ahead.
I splash this water upon you,
feeling the rock-face crumble
and, falling, I offer
that each moment I breathe
the water searches me,
that every step you take
may touch the shore.

NEGOTIATIONS FOR WARMTH

Like the politician after battle,
I rummage the slashbin,
afraid of what I'll find.
The choice is limited
to expendable waste,
to slivers and limbs.
Sympathy for the fallen
gets laughs here at the mill,
where sawdust delights the sawyer.
He celebrates the carnage;
"O, shit!," he says
with the thrill of it,
plank by plank.
The slash is left
for the hands of cold scavengers.
So I condole the dead
and pick at the leavings:
diplomacy while looting the slain.

WINTER SONG

The new pines have drowned in the field.
They lie on the mud like swatches of rust.
Rain falls so heavily
it stands frozen in the dark
and I fear for the horses in the field
weighed down by it,
for the field itself
scored of any life
by the broad whip of the rain.
Bringing in the animals,
I trip and fall.
I had hoped for a brighter end.
Something public—
a last wave and a leap,
perhaps, from some famous bridge.
But the mud pulls at my hands
like blades sucked in
for a sodden death.
My last words will freeze.
Their charm will come out gagged.
Embroidered with dark frost,
I make small efforts at escape
and grasp the field.

A POEM FOR CHRIST

Smoke from the silent mill
belies the holiday.
Somebody's at work.
Not the fields, who give their trees
cold sap for the celebration;
not the trees, who chain the air.
Christmas Day to New Year's—
the dead of winter.
Still, there is something for Christ,
though dead as a doornail
and out-Judased by The Church.
The mill oddly graces this valley
on this day only.
There is value in cold walls.
The path of smoke lights the morning
so that God's words are written,
for the moment,
grey against grey.

But, like Christ,
December will die out.
What's the use?
Unless the mud take us,
warm us,
couple with our blood and body
for the sake of passage
from this year to the next.

INFANT SORROW

Poets pry open the words
to take as much as they can,
gorge them so they spill,
while careless children say
whatever the hell they like.
Another night of silence for us both.
I walk from rug to rug,
each scrap of paper filled
with ink and arrows
and rubbed-out words,
and you disintegrate before me
with a pleasant dead smile.
Your mind is gorged
with small electrocutions.
It will happen now.
Several times each day it will.
You've so suddenly grown ill,
you fall like the aged
through each long day.
There's little to do.
As fathers go,
I've done my best—
a useless pleasantry
when the roots of illness
tighten in your brain
and take the brain with it
where they grow,
dark and sickened.
It is blocked from its emergence
to language and light
by an unexpected freeze.

So we sit in silence
and sulk through Mother Goose,
as though reading of Jack and Jill,
of Cripple Dick upon a stick
and the giant Jack could kill,
we'd deny the dead and the sick.

Yet here I lay my silence down
(hating it and holding him)
to match the silence of my son.
Conceived in laughter, on a whim,

and now he's ill. He shrieks without
the slightest meaning in his speech.
His hands caress his open mouth
and nothing comes within his reach.

LARGESSE IN LATE WINTER

Sap means little to the mud.
It is a pliant goo
to be frozen with the rest.
It lights the grass' way
through the dead earth,
a small release
to mark the end of winter.
Though the ice wars
with such births,
summer is assured,
for the tentative announcement of the leaf
shoulders the earth aside.

ON AN IMAGINED SNAPSHOT

(for Jakob Hofland)

who steps from the photo just
two minutes
into his life.
He grasps the nearest finger,
girding against the years
he'll spend in special hospitals
watching the young expire.
My sister wrote of the "oh"
she uttered upon his birth,
the surprising depth of it.
She grasps him like the air the earth,
while I, the wellmeaning uncle,
look on through letters,
through conjurations of the baby ward.
O, I know neither hands nor eyes,
know only that his grace takes my breath,
in measure of such words as these.

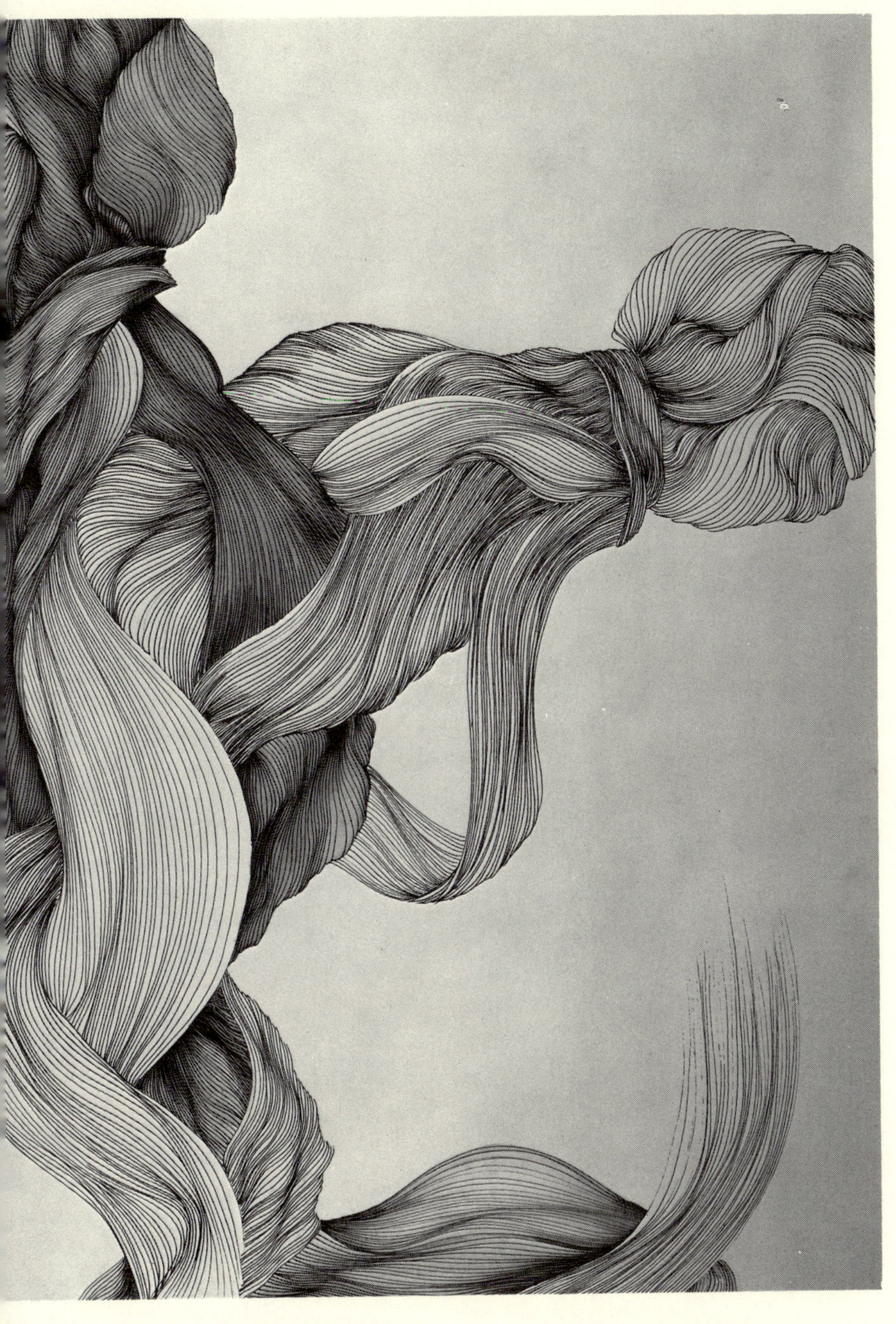

KITCHEN MEMORIALS

The scrape of the door
hardly matters to them;
no sudden halt against the danger.
Rather, the roar of breadcrusts
down fairways of bugs,
the high applause of mice—
all of it—
spiders rattling their webs,
red and black ants
voracious for the sweet,
the noise of eat and drink,
of glut behind the sugar bowl.

April brings the residents,
who with brooms clarify each corner.
They tiptoe through the carnage,
appalled by the audacity of rats,
and end the winter with rags.
Over cocktails,
they pat each others' backs
for being so pleasantly clean,
clean despite the leavings in the kitchen:

a bottle of Alhambra Spring Water,
dewy hearse for one rat—

six drawers of small black crescents—

a circle of crumbs,
wherein was a round of bread,
borne away whole by the ants.

DINNER AT EIGHT

The talk grows loud and fast
and fades. Well well,
the poet passes out
and dreams in a sturdy chair,
excused from talking
by the kind and drunken guests . . .
dreams of fear,
not of monsters and bugs,
but of words badly put.
The mot juste thumbs its nose.
The struggle for it fails,
too quietly for the pain it's caused.
It gives way to speechlessness,
a northern spot
where vines dry in the snow.
Would that I could hope for the best,
that phrases would jump from the gullet,
all washed down with the reddest cabernet.
But left alone and cold,
left in the kitchen at 4AM,
I wake to the clutter and bones,
stiff in the black morning.

LUMINOUS DETAILS

The morning arrives in the guise of warmth
and we freeze on the riverbank,
undressed in our haste for summer.
In such ways,
we are stunned in April.
Difficult to turn a phrase;
the light points up the weakness of speech,
when a word of explanation
gets lost in the emergence of leaves.

It is wise to stick to details:
the root warmed by light
in the ice-ringed morning.
The intensities of growth insist
we start out simply,
cold mud the beginning
to the certainty of spring.

THE FALLING SICKNESS

I

The smile appears
and distances us.
I make preparations—
without alarm—
clear away the chairs,
make a place for you,
take guard by the stove
so you will not thrash against it,
and await the seizure's start.
You are struck from your feet
and dark glides up your body.
Help does no good.
You accede to it
as you would to a faulty plug.

Light scores the wall.
The curtains hang in it
and it grids the floor
where you are thrown.
I'm told you hear nothing
and recall nothing,
a hole in the darkness
from hour to hour.
Your eyes ascend to your brain,
as if to view its bad connections.

II

We watch his play
as though he were infirm
on the jungle jims.
We seek solace in medical texts.
We look to the Greeks,
would tell of their love of lost minds,
how the worshipful boy
in the midst of a fit
received the oracle.

Or Joan of Arc at Orleans
stunned before battle.
Of Dostoevsky luminous and cramped.

But his ears are blocked
by the fit that stiffens him.
The doctor assures us with technical drugs.
I fear his smiles,
for he's at a loss,
a healthy man
in awe of helplessness.

III

We build up schedules
of breakfast and lunch.
Work sees us through to 5 PM.
We make plans and clean the house,
grow successful
like everybody else.

I sit in silence at my desk,
finding the glow of comfort not enough,
not enough three meals a day
and a good mind.
The brain grows hard as it fails,
its thoughts like slivers
glinting
on the edge of a stone.
Nothing cures it. Not its comforts,
its success or self-esteem.
A common problem, I think,
though there's no help from the others.
Profound depression.
It comes from almost everything—
darkness over morning toast,
the name in lights,
one's small betrayals of wife or friends.
Rightfully ours, no matter what.
I search a way to say it!
No nothing.

IV

You form words in your hands
and try them out in silence.
Nothing comes,
though you shape the air so artfully.
When I help,
forming my lips in the proper way,
you seem to fail:
you look for a toy,
wait for me to stop.
I worry how words elude you,
though I know how it is.
Language never comes.
It must be wrenched from the throat
like food from an arid field.
I gather all my strength
for a well-turned phrase
and it fails on the page.
I scratch it out and try again.
I blot my hands with ink,
failure after failure.

I drag a line from all this
like light from a hole—
the best words.
They appear by chance,
a clear mark pulled from the black,
like the word or two
you force from your silence.

V

We lie on the kitchen floor
embraced in the sun
like lovers stiff in one another's arms.
Your body folds and you sleep,
exhausted by such excess,
knowing that I held you
and watched you leave
in your solitary trance,
yet held you
as you danced in it.

UPON BEING A GOOD SPORT

In spring,
the tennis players vault the net
shouting "deuce" and "love."
Such civility,
though I fear that, shaking hands,
I'll lay waste my opponent
with a left to the chin.
I look kind in white
and congratulate my foe
for a convincing shot,
but I rob my victory—
of rage,
of gloating for the pillaged prize.
Rather, elegance and smiles,
the certainty that tennis tears no wounds.

So we play,
while in spring the fern unravels,
its fingers stiffened in the morning ice.
The dew boils the leaf
and we lift ourselves from dinner
as if from war.

COCKTAILS IN SPRING

This is the night for bitter affections
at sundown on a porch,
for jokes about misspent youth,
when for the sake of hanging one on,
such grey extremes were reached.
The sun sets on my in-laws
and the insistent booze convinces me
I've gone nuts in the dusk.
I fall to the spiked grass,
amazed by its passage through my limbs,
by the spiny leaves,
dichondra's push,
by the slice of new blades
through watered and slushy rot,
by the disintegration and soak of each bone.

The lesson of a spring afternoon.
I make a sodden return to talk,
once again a barrel of fun at cocktail time,
stalked by the trees
over bourbon and lies.

WEEDING AND WATERING
(for Pepperwood, California)

I

Flood washed the forest floor
of the clutch of dead trees.
But, high waters glut the nuance;
in spring the details were gone.
No sun-felled sorrel.
No webs for the fly's fragile tomb.
Just the redwoods pulling from the mud
against columns of fallen light.

II

The path to the forest turns
to view these recollections
that floods come and go.
The tourist searching ravages
finds only foundations,
a former house or store,
the survivors of the great flood of '64.
Residents are confident,
farming corn between deluges.
They eye the river from their mobile homes,
expectant of the worst,
as when it glutted the hills
and tree trunks skewered railroads,
whole frame houses cresting on the tide.
The last farmland borders the forest.
Its entrance is badly marked,
a hole in the treeline
at the back of a plain of weeds.
But, one knows the details:
the clutch of fire and brush;
sorrel weed broken by light;
abandoned webs,
and the upward swirl of the sequoia sempiveren.

LAST EVENING

Last evening,
though I hung myself in strips,
drawn on the porch
so the moon burned the bits,
my elbows nailed to the roof,
my eyes to termite nests,
I asked forgiveness
only to get on with coffee.
The argument was inconvenient, you see.
I finally lost the fight,
though a twin for Bette Davis.
Such prices I pay
for the moments I intend,
as this morning
when the chair slid away
and left me puddled on the linoleum,
your shouts like knives
in my dissemblings.
I apologize.
My truths are broom straws
in a dirty house.
Their appearance makes for pain,
like the kitchen window
opening on an old view.

JUNE 21

We danced like summer ghosts
in the firelight.
The wine fell from us in such sweat
that we grew slick
in the well-stoked flames.
Too much booze on solstice night
and we waste the day in the orchard
in recovery.
The apples knell our distress.
Spearmint rises on the morning heat
to salve the gorged heads.
We've saved ourselves once more.

SAW

(for Edmunds Bunkse)

The sawmill workers dance in their boots
with the barkeep and her mother
and my brother-in-law has said
he quits.
Thus he lounges on the white line in the road
and sings the Latvian National Anthem.

He sings of the sawyer
binding trees to the cradle
to rip them lengthwise.
It takes no time at all.
They come to their end relieved
of encumbrance such as branch and sap.
He rejoices each layer of skin
peeled back by the saw,
the glistening juice on the blade.

I leave him for the mill,
jealous of such moments,
the saw a faint circle
among stacks of ageing wood.
Its teeth can pierce skin,
leaving oily holes in the hands,
a flow of blood to gore the cradle.
Noting each trunk of Douglas Fir
stacked for ravishing in the morning,
I help the saw to the task,
offering my throat
for its evening pleasure.

As usual, the loggers brawl.
Only the voice in the road
insists we've failed of our ends,
so I help him to his feet.
We are lessons in the worth
of getting loaded together,
led to our beds past the shipping lot
where the boards are stacked to dry.

EPITAPH, FOR A HORSE THAT RAN INTO A TREE

Here lies a laughable death,
having blazed a trail one inch—
of no moment to his last breath;
of none since.

May he rest in peace,
who trundled past the forgotten gate
all bones and fat, one breath released
from fenced boredom and great age.

THE GOOD OLD DAYS

Farm kids, as they will,
thrill one another in the hay.
A fine diversion,
though the cows have been doing it for years.
The rotting wood deepens the play
of nosing each other in the dark
and gives it the feel of old seasons,
when a good obsession
seemed the natural thing to do.
Lust was scheduled
by the appearance of leaves.
Not then the yearly task
of rutting for the farmer's good.
No bearing young
for the profits to be made
in powdered milk.

But the cow is dim,
especially in matters of love.
No imagination,
and now they find their fun
in a whirl of cud
and feed each day.
The good old days
diffuse in the barn's dark,
surviving only in the laughter
and the underwear
in the corner in the hay.

AUGUST

Floods rearrange this river.
Winters are noted for their sound:
a roar of water in the dark.
Spring dries out the forest
and cracks the broken wood.
The fog rises to the sun
and dries as it goes
so that in summer
we may fry by the riverside.

Disregarding tender skin,
I leave my clothes on a branch
and roll in the water on the shore.
The sun burns and burns
with small regard for buttocks
or available shade.
I curl like paper
in my peeling skin
and await the moment
when August will have its day.

For here it is a pleasing month,
allowing even ecstasy
on certain afternoons.
We give in with ease.
It's good to do it here in the sun
where we can see our exchange,
how the light makes it clear.
Dirt shadows your back,
where muscle turns to ridge,
your belly to moss
grown thick from the floods this winter.

A union to accomodate the seasons.
In August the seed gains strength
for a moment of growth,
second by second
to escape to the heat.

POEM

The dark path
turns grey across the creekbed,
grey in the clearings.
It gives faint direction
to an evening walk.
Bad news to lose the way.
We go blind in the Old Orchard,
lost on familiar ground.

WATER

The spring falls from the broken pipe.
We climb the hill to this minor source,
in hopes that its short run
will offer words for the failing light,
while far below
water from a brackish well
speeds through pumps
to quench the residents.
Trillium die in our fingers
on the way back.
They will not recover,
despite the ministrations
of water in a glass.
Hard work for water,
to cleanse and cure
and steep the earth as well.
But I do not worship the dirt.
To the prayerful and sublime
I offer that a tree is nothing special,
that it grows just as it should.
Water eases a passage,
repairs a break.
Enough to say of it
that it does what it can.

We climb the hill,
hurried by the late afternoon,
and sit with wet throats
beside the eroded spring,
conversant and refreshed.

IDENTIFYING THE DEAD

A barn like this shelters ancient pains.
Hearts and bones have failed here for years,
despite the kindly vet
and our assumption that
we'll all be alive forever.
The wood smells of dead animals.
I've secured myself against darkness
and dark fears,
but I'm afraid to die,
to go out gracefully
like the old horse
felled by a heart attack.
He is piled up in his stall
like sticks.
I search his eye for some Truth,
nudge it with the muddy boot.
Nothing.
Mud and piss mix on the floor
in the old well-known smell.
We are black and empty in the dark
and dying like all the rest,
sharing our blood with the bugs,
alive and dead,
giving them what they need
to eat to couple and excite.

SUMMER LIGHT

The narrow-winged damsel fly
couples in the air.
This is a minor detail,
a flurry of blue light
in ecstasy across the field.
The redwoods grow thick in the wind.
The horses chew the grass.
Dull lives,
insensitive to small pleasures,
like love in the bright light,
in mid-air.

LUCIDITY

The river breaks in the light
and we laugh at our scattered bodies,
how they waver in the filtered sun.
He swims with us,
no longer ill,
though his view is still in shreds,
like that of a fish thrown back
from a long run on a hook.
His first laugh in years
brings up guffaws from the closed throat.
He laughs again and again,
too new at it to know
the subtleties of a good joke.
His voice has rarely
risen high or humorous
in any quest for eloquence.
Never like this moment
when, dazed by the sun,
he shouts at the source
of light and recognition.

HARVEST

As the plums bloody our lips,
leaving us senseless in the heat,
we sun ourselves
on the parched and sharpened grass.
Certain of the moment,
the leaf, its edge turned sear, chills.
We find in this irony
the truth of the season's change,
how quiet its killing.
It comes, as they say,
in good time,
when death has already come,
surrounded us, carried the day,
when rain gathers silently
in the hot sky.

EARLY FALL

I

Sap struggles an inch and gives up.
The pears have quit.
These trees are standing firewood,
not much else,
old sticks borne up from habit
whose few bits of fruit feed the spiders.
I am filled with admiration,
for webs drape from them
like crinoline
and I climb the trees
for a closer look.

The spiders find me out.
I fall through the branches,
tear the webs.
Swirling around the orchard,
I am a pillar for the spiders,
excretion head to foot.

II

Where I crawl,
brittle with fast-drying goo,
a cross-hatch lines the orchard.
The string pulls from my groin
with slight tears.
I beat the ground with a convulsive switch.
I am the last word in lace.

SPARE TIME

The clock's pause at six pm
reminds me that, like the Hindenburgh,
this evening will pass away.
Thus the worth of giving in.
I have only arguments for the flesh,
for seizure and glut,
for time will dry us out soon enough.

Why refuse me?
Witness this Fall,
how the fruit pulls from the trees.
You say they die comfortably,
a natural end.
But their fall is like ours:
separate pears rotting separately.
Private enough, such death,
though wasteful of the crop.

True! They lie
in clumps for comfort.
And so should we.
They share their warmth,
so that they savor into March
their crowded end,
a fine embrace across the field
of pear with pear with pear.

But refuse if you wish.
Just recall
that I pillage my mind
for an assurance of youth
and sample each alternative.
Even a pact with the devil
brings too little too late.

The joints will fix.
The slow loss of sense,
year to year,
will leave us screwy on the porch,
and time, after tea,
will get you, and me.

COLLOQUY

The pear's break from the branch
proves the farmer's adage that
by fall whatever grows is grown.
We lie in the Old Orchard,
surrounded by these grasses
which ride the earth like fine whips.
Soliloquies are slurred,
the pleasures of bad wine after dinner
damned to bad language
and the sun fails behind a tree.
"I am true," I say.
"True as the winter is long."
Your breath is regular,
an orderly grace against my conviction
that you don't believe a word.
Who would?
The pears fill with flesh
and fall with the apples and plums.
Hyperbole salts the cut.
Yet I justify and justify
while each breath falls silent and,
in rut, the squirrels turn stone.

ODIOUS TASKS

(apologies to Robert Herrick)

Beneath this roof such rounds of shit,
there is no escape from it.
A mist of bugs obscures the light,
reminding me that when I cite
the cow as kind, the horse as king,
I cite the source of all these things.
O, aided by the broom's caress,
Shovel!, bring me peace and rest
and clear a trail from stall to trough
for ammonia's hope to clean it off.
Rid yourself of prejudice.
We should not balk at tasks like this;
though death, in customary form,
finds filth a friend to hungry worms,
I prefer a cleaner path
to dinner and a bath.
And if we lag, the barn will fill
with leavings, hay, with bits of swill
and us, the workhands, finally dead,
lastly, safely buried.

AWAITING THE END OF OCTOBER 31

Our teeth blur with talk
for the fallen apples rot with Halloween.
There are no children here
to dress in death's guise,
to bring about assurances that
really these things are myths,
false threats sealed in Hershey Bars.
The oak reveals a shade in every leaf.
My rake has scraped them in piles.
Still they come.
I've burned them; they fall.
I would defend myself,
lacking only the verve
and a proper weapon:
shibboleths and garlic won't do
against the severed leaf.
One last look at the glutted field
and we wind ourselves in our sheets.

CORDWOOD

(for Charles Daly)

I

The wood here surrounds me
like legs and elbows gathered
in a pile.
The sap searches its canal,
though lumpen on the shaved stumps.
I pick them apart, searching
the right age and size,
straight grain the test
of a well-wrought piece.
Sap turns the corners,
abused by the flames;
it browns like butter in a pan,
ashed finally.
One makes stories of it,
from the knuckled, stuck-out turnings
of each log piled on another,
so that the perfect fire has grace beyond its flames.

II

In winter,
mud oozes ice.
Very few talk of it.
My words clatter to the ground,
like glass,
the caustic nettle of moss
breaks in the wind,
and I freeze dead in my tracks everywhere.
Agreeing with my father-in-law
on the worth of a sharpened axe,
I hone the blade for a destructive edge.

"A dull one'll do the job," he says.
"But you need precision."
Odd to insist on it,
when there's little sparkle
in a bucked log.

My cold shoes disappear
in the light of sparks
from the grinding wheel.
I love the moment
when the axe gets the wood;
especially those with knots.
It takes real muscle,
though a good edge eases the axe's passage,
so that the wood will give before I do.

III

A platform for the quartering,
the chopping block fawns;
it is a trustie.
Each block has a name.
One I had was called Julius.
They give it to themselves,
thus the lie to themselves,
for a name gathers the truth
and Julius was just a piece of wood,
like the others.
The block leans, lurches,
so that every piece of wood placed on it
falls over, placed again and falls.
For the axeman's burden,
it doesn't give a goddamn.
One day I'll put a blade through my foot.

IV

The bare oak sits witness,
from which are strung two cloth fish,
Made in Japan.
In summer they twirl for the leaves,
drawing from the poplars belly laughs.
Winter sees them hang,
examples for the wood,
the blade and me:
a criminal bunch.
The raised axe borders a last circle,
the blade held up on a last bit of air,
before the fall.

V

The executioner's axe has the virtue
of being human-soaked, humanized.
Ask after the dark masked practitioner;
see how he likes his work.
The dead head bows,
a little flip of skin
easing its drop to the bucket.
It is, the executioner says, simple.
So if my head bounces side to side,
a little lump in the metal trough,
I wish it gently held—
like Leon Trotsky's,
who got one in the brain,
Guillotine his own best test.
Marie-Antoinette beheaded,
Mishima ungutted,
Custer dehaired.
So much for a probable future.
Dead necks and thoughts go
with the same alacrity.

Blood marks on the axe are my last say,
the one thing given
and grudgingly spit away,
my cry at the end like a joke
that lays them in the aisles,
leaving only a cutting edge,
an edge
to cut my words free,
now.

I fall in pieces from the block
and water the fire pit with the glazed,
the last departings from my throat.
Strange to say, it's summer.
The leaves take sap.
Young lovers feel each other up in the sun
and the trees leap from the earth.

VI

I wish that I had done
more before this moment,
not allowed myself
such freedoms to do nothing.
I have possessed few clear things.
So I grasp what I can.
The heat consumes me,
useless now to the tree
this cold winter.
Though I search for light,
none approaches this,
in this kindling wood.

Terence Clarke lives in San Francisco with his wife, Cathleen Daly, and their son, Brennan.